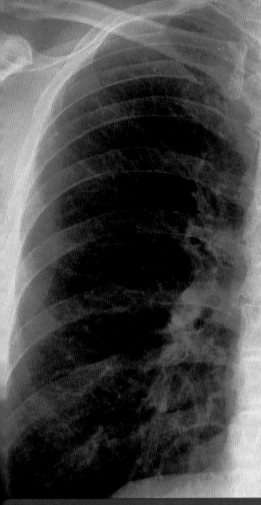

THE SWEYNE JUN...
Keary Road
Swanscombe
Kent
DA10 0PU
Tel: 01322 383296

Skeletons

INSIDE and OUT

By Claire Daniel

Series Literacy Consultant
Dr Ros Fisher

Pearson Education Limited
Edinburgh Gate
Harlow
Essex CM20 2JE
England

www.longman.co.uk

ISBN 0 582 8454 16

Colour reproduction by Colourscan, Singapore
Printed and bound in China by Leo Paper Products Ltd.

The Publisher's policy is to use paper manufactured from sustainable forests.

10 9 8 7 6 5 4 3

The following people from **DK** have
contributed to the development of this product:

Art Director Rachael Foster

Ross George, Carole Oliver **Design**	**Managing Editor** Scarlett O'Hara
Helen McFarland **Picture Research**	**Editorial** Nada Jolic
Richard Czapnik, Andy Smith **Cover Design**	**Production** Rosalind Holmes
David Burnie **Consultant**	**DTP** David McDonald

Dorling Kindersley would like to thank: Clive Savage for additional design work, Rose Horridge in the DK Picture Library and
Johnny Pau for additional cover design work.

Picture Credits: Alamy Images: Brandon Cole Marine Photography 24car; Martin Ruegner 11cb. Ardea London Ltd: Pascal Goetgheluck 26b.
Corbis: 28-29b. DK Images: Phillip Dowell 9tcr; Oxford University Museum 3tcr, 19bl; Jerry Young 25tr. Getty Images: Tim Davis 12t; Steve
Shatsushek 25br. Masterfile UK: Min Roman 5t. Nature Picture Library: Tony Heald 17b. Photolibrary.com: 14b. Science Photo Library: Roger Harris
6r; Alfred Pasieka 1, 7tr. Warren Photographic: 23br.

All other images: DK Dorling Kindersley © 2004. For further information see www.dkimages.com
Dorling Kindersley Ltd., 80 Strand, London WC2R 0RL

Contents

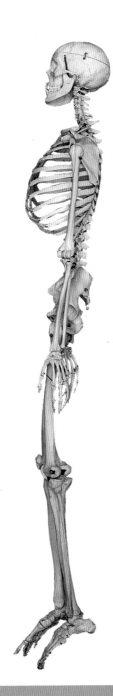

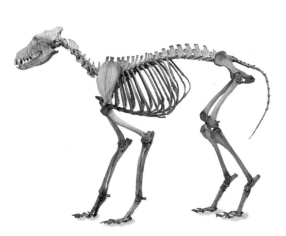

All About Skeletons

A skeleton is a hard framework of bones.
It supports the body's weight and gives it shape.
It protects the soft parts inside the body. It also
works with muscles to help the body move.

Skeletons work differently in different
animals. In **mammals**, birds and many other
animals, the skeleton is a framework made of
bones inside the skin. A skeleton on the inside
of the body is called an **endoskeleton**.

This boy's skeleton helps him
move in all sorts of ways.

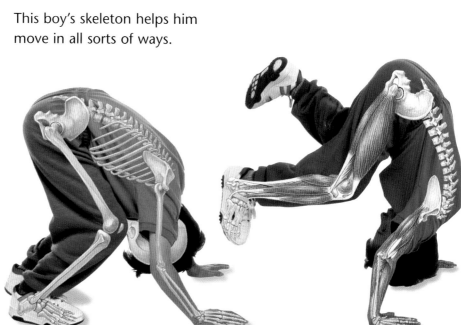

When the exoskeleton becomes too small, the crab crawls out of it.

In other animals, the skeleton is a hard covering outside the body. This is called an **exoskeleton**. A crab or a beetle shell is an exoskeleton.

An exoskeleton protects and supports the animal's body like an endoskeleton. However, some exoskeletons cannot expand as an animal grows. When this happens, an animal must shed its old exoskeleton and grow a new, larger one.

A beetle's exoskeleton protects its body.

The Human Skeleton

How do humans move around? Without a skeleton, your body would be floppy and shapeless, like a blob of jelly. You wouldn't be able to stand up, sit down, run or walk. However, the human body has a skeleton. It is made up of bones that work together with muscles to make movement possible. These bones also protect the body and keep its soft parts safe. Let's take a look at how parts of the human skeleton work to protect and support the body.

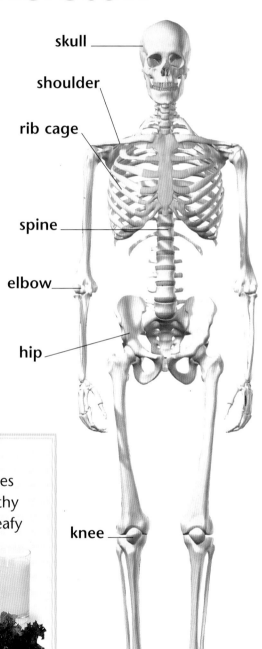

skull

shoulder

rib cage

spine

elbow

hip

knee

foot

Growing Bones

Your bones grow as you grow. Your bones need calcium and exercise to grow healthy and strong. Milk, cheese, yoghurt and leafy green vegetables are high in calcium. Your body also needs Vitamin D to help it absorb calcium. Milk and cereals have Vitamin D added to them.

What Your Bones Protect

The ribs form a cage that guards the heart and lungs. The ribs are connected to the **sternum**.

The **skull** protects the brain. Without protection, even a small bump on the head might damage the brain inside the skull. The only part of the skull that moves is the jawbone. It allows you to open your mouth and chew food.

x-ray photo

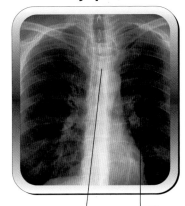

sternum / rib

In this x-ray photo, you can see how the ribs curve around the chest.

Did You Know?

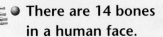

- There are 206 bones in an adult's skeleton.
- An adult has 12 pairs of ribs that curve around the sides of the chest.
- There are 14 bones in a human face.

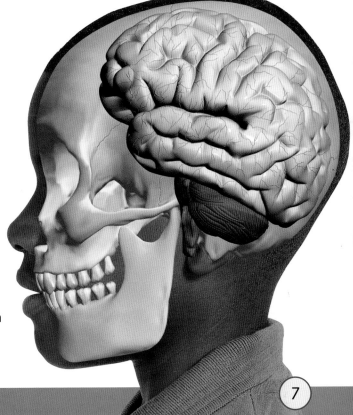

A human skull protects the brain and four sense organs: the eyes, ears, nose and tongue.

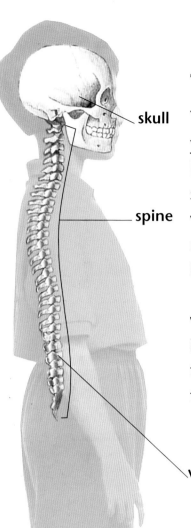
skull

spine

vertebra

The Spine

Your **spine** holds your body upright when you sit, stand or walk. It's also called the backbone, but it's not just one bone. The spine is made up of many small bones called **vertebrae**. Each vertebra moves, which makes the spine flexible. It allows us to bend in different directions.

Inside the spine, there is the spinal cord, which contains nerves. These nerves carry information, such as sensations from the body, to the brain. They also carry commands from the brain to parts of the body.

These gymnasts rely on their spines for support.

Movement and the Spine

Humans walk on two legs, so the spine is vertical. Animals that walk on four legs have a horizontal spine. Many animals that swim, such as fish and whales, also have horizontal spines.

vertical spine

horizontal spine

Twisting and Bending

Our bones are connected by **joints**. They allow the skeleton to bend, twist and turn. Some joints allow the bones to move forwards and backwards. These joints are called hinge joints and are found in the knees and elbows.

Other joints allow the bones to move around in a circle. These are called ball-and-socket joints and are found in the hips, shoulders and between the first and second vertebra in your neck.

ball-and-socket joint

hinge joint

Your Bones at Work

Leg bones carry your weight as you stand, walk, run and jump. Humans move on two legs, which leaves the arms free to do other things.

Hand bones allow you to pick a flower or hold tightly onto a rope. You can grasp and grip because you have opposable thumbs. This means the thumb can move freely and touch the tips of your fingers.

An opposable thumb helps humans hold many things.

A runner uses different bones and **joints** to go from kneeling to running.

Mammal and Bird Skeletons

Animals such as cats, whales and bats are **mammals**. They have skeletons that help them move. Mammal skeletons vary in size and shape.

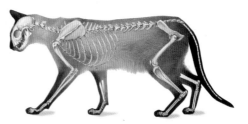

a cat skeleton

A cat's skeleton is built for walking and climbing. Its **spine** bends easily. Unlike cats, a whale's skeleton is built for gliding under water. A whale has muscles that move its lower spine up and down in a wave-like movement. The muscle also moves its tail fins up and down to push itself forwards.

a killer whale

a whale skeleton

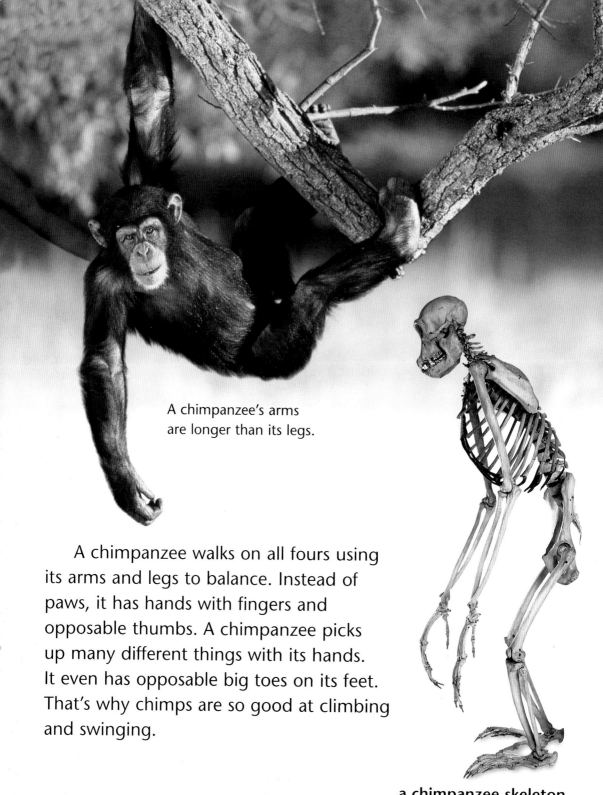

A chimpanzee's arms
are longer than its legs.

A chimpanzee walks on all fours using
its arms and legs to balance. Instead of
paws, it has hands with fingers and
opposable thumbs. A chimpanzee picks
up many different things with its hands.
It even has opposable big toes on its feet.
That's why chimps are so good at climbing
and swinging.

a chimpanzee skeleton

An elephant's leg bones are strong, but lightweight, because of the spongy bone inside.

an African elephant

An elephant has thick, strong leg bones and flat toe bones that hold up its huge body. It also has strong neck **vertebrae** to support its heavy head. This support allows the elephant to reach out its trunk to drink, grasp food and spray water over its body.

A giraffe has long, thin legs that support its body and long neck. A giraffe's neck is also very flexible so it can eat off the ground as easily as eating from the tops of trees.

Giraffes can grow to a height of 5.5 metres. A giraffe's neck can be up to 2 metres long.

Did You Know?

A giraffe has seven neck vertebrae – the same number as a human. Its vertebrae are just bigger than ours.

A horse's skeleton is built for running.

A horse has long, strong leg bones. Large muscles connect the leg bones to other bones in its skeleton. The muscles have room to flex, which gives horses the power to move their front and back legs. This helps horses to gallop and jump.

A kangaroo has an amazing ability to jump. Its skeleton is designed to stay fairly upright as it jumps along. Its long back feet and tail help it to balance.

A kangaroo's skeleton is designed for jumping.

Bats share many of the same features as birds. Bats and birds look different on the outside. However, both have bones that are strong and light. This is so they can easily lift their bodies off the ground to fly.

A bat's wings are made of skin that is stretched over four long finger bones. It also has many small bones and **joints** in its feet that help it to grasp and hang onto a perch.

A bat is the only flying mammal.

Did You Know?

Most bats' thumbs have a single claw that is used for climbing, crawling or holding food.

a bat skeleton

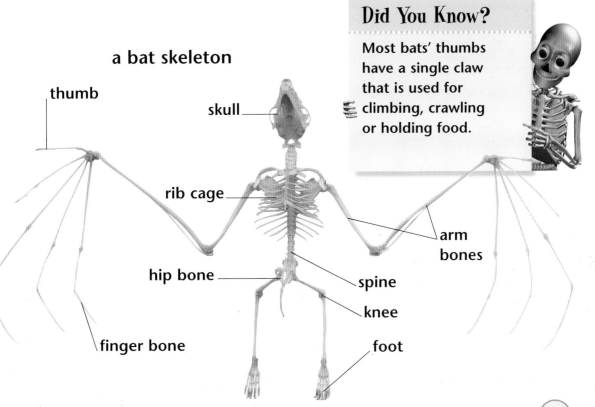

thumb

skull

rib cage

arm bones

hip bone

spine

knee

finger bone

foot

Most birds' skeletons are made up of many hollow bones with tiny air sacs to keep them light.

A bird has a beak for eating and grasping food. It also has a large **sternum**, or breastbone. This holds their powerful wing-flapping muscles in place.

Eurasian jay

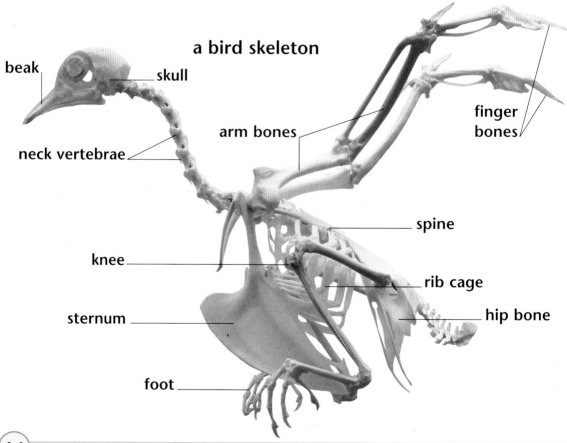

a bird skeleton

beak

skull

arm bones

finger bones

neck vertebrae

spine

knee

rib cage

sternum

hip bone

foot

Reptile and Amphibian Skeletons

Reptiles and **amphibians** have **endoskeletons** like **mammals**. Their endoskeletons help them move around on land and sometimes in the water. Reptiles and amphibians also have **skulls** and **spines**, and most have legs and tails.

A crocodile is a reptile. It has strong jawbones and teeth built for gripping prey of all sizes. Short, sturdy leg bones make it quick on land. Almost half of a crocodile's **vertebrae** are in its long, thick tail. It uses its tail as a powerful paddle to move quickly through water.

Exploring Fossils

Animal bones from the past tell us a lot about how creatures lived. In ancient rocks, scientists have found **fossils** of **extinct** reptiles, such as dinosaurs. Scientists compare ancient bones to bones of animals living today to discover the differences.

A crocodile is fast on land and in water because of its strong skeleton.

a crocodile fossil

Amazing Turtles

Turtles and tortoises have both **endoskeletons** and **exoskeletons**. Their hard shells are exoskeletons that protect their soft internal organs and the internal endoskeleton. These animals can hide their heads and limbs inside their hard shells when frightened by a predator.

a tortoise skeleton

A snake depends on many tiny flexible **vertebrae** to move. Its vertebrae allow it to move in many different directions. A large snake can have up to 400 vertebrae in its spine, with a pair of ribs attached to almost every one.

a snake skeleton

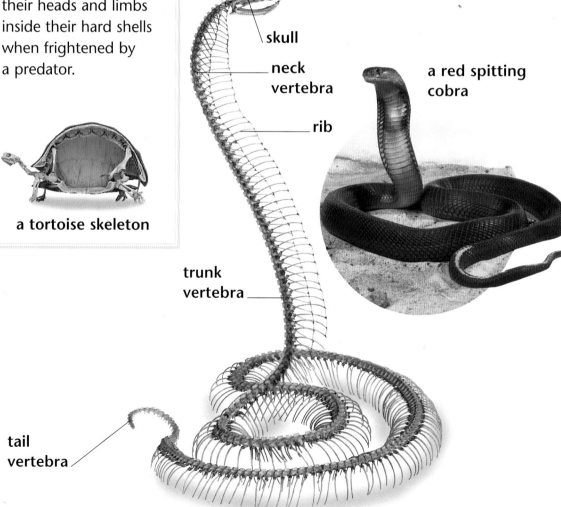

skull

neck vertebra

rib

a red spitting cobra

trunk vertebra

tail vertebra

Amphibians, such as frogs and toads, have an endoskeleton that helps them move in and out of water. A frog's endoskeleton helps it to push up off its strong, springy back legs. Frogs don't have ribs. This allows them to land on their chests without breaking any bones.

Another amphibian called the salamander, has a strong, bony endoskeleton. Its skeleton and well-developed muscles help it move easily, both on land and in the water. To move fast, a salamander sways its body. To leap, it flexes and straightens its tail.

tiger salamander

frog skeleton

finger bone

skull

arm bone

vertebra

spine

toe bone

leg bone

hip

Strong leg muscles and webbed feet give a frog power to jump from place to place.

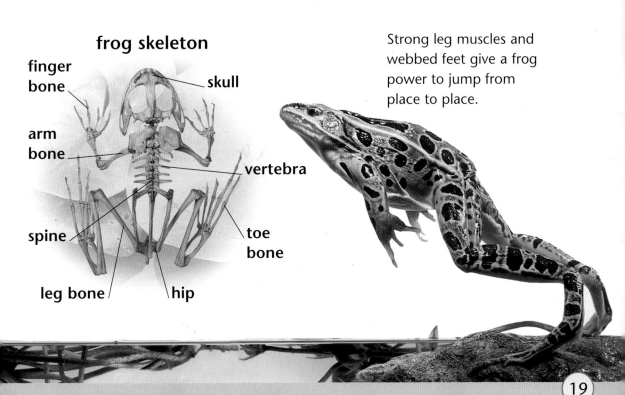

Sea-creature Skeletons

Sea creatures have different kinds of skeletons. Some, such as fish, have **endoskeletons** with ribs and spines. Others, such as crabs, have hard **exoskeletons**.

Sea-creature Endoskeletons

Most fish have endoskeletons made of bone. A fish's skeleton has a **skull**, a **spine** and ribs. Its sleek shape helps it move quickly through the water. Muscles pull on each side of the spine, bending the fish's body and tail from side to side, pushing it forwards. Fin bones help the fish balance, steer and move along.

carp

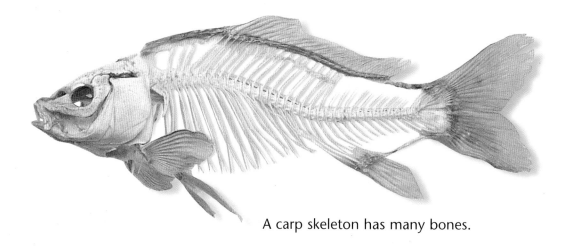

A carp skeleton has many bones.

Some fish, such as sharks and rays, have skeletons made of **cartilage** instead of bone. Cartilage is a strong flexible tissue. Part of your nose is supported by cartilage.

The great white shark's spine is made of cartilage. It stretches from the tip of its tail to the base of its skull. Each fin has rods of firm but flexible cartilage, which help it keep its shape. Its fins help it to dive through the water and change direction quickly. They also stop a shark from rolling over.

a shark's jaw

Both the shark's upper and lower jaws move forwards to grab its prey.

a great white shark

Sea-creature Exoskeletons

Sea creatures with **exoskeletons** often move differently from those with **endoskeletons**. A starfish has an exoskeleton that is not very flexible. It moves on tiny tube feet. These feet have suction cups that slowly pull the starfish along.

A sea urchin's shell is covered with stiff **spines**. This exoskeleton helps the sea urchin defend itself from creatures that might want to eat it or step on it. Like the starfish, the sea urchin moves on tiny tube feet. Its spines also help. At the base of each spine is a ball-and-socket **joint**. This allows the spines to move in all directions.

Did You Know?

A sea urchin may look like a furry ball, but it is not. Its spines are sharp and pointed. Stepping on a sea urchin's exoskeleton is very painful.

sea urchin

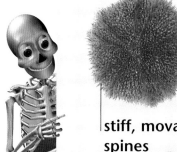

stiff, movable spines

starfish

Crabs, lobsters and shrimps are **crustaceans**. Their hard exoskeleton covers their legs and bodies. As crustaceans grow, they moult, or shed, their exoskeletons. They grow new exoskeletons to fit their growing bodies.

Crustaceans have legs and arms, called limbs. They use most of these limbs to move about. Some crustaceans have pincers, or grasping claws, that they use to defend themselves. Joints connect their limbs and body parts, which makes them flexible. That is why most crustaceans move easily.

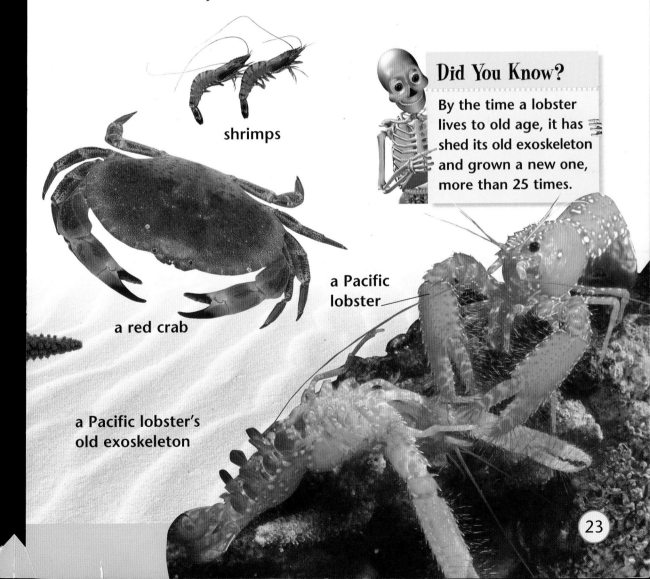

shrimps

Did You Know?

By the time a lobster lives to old age, it has shed its old exoskeleton and grown a new one, more than 25 times.

a red crab

a Pacific lobster

a Pacific lobster's old exoskeleton

23

A scallop's **exoskeleton** is made up of two half shells that are shaped like fans. These shells are held together by a hinge. One large muscle opens and closes the hinges. Most of the time, a scallop lies on the ocean floor. To move, it opens and closes its shell quickly. This forces water out of the shell near the hinge and drives it forwards.

Did You Know?

Some animals, such as jellyfish, don't have skeletons. Water supports their soft bodies including their organs.

a purple jellyfish

queen scallops

Arachnid and Insect Skeletons

Arachnids have two-part bodies and eight walking legs. Insects, like ladybirds, have bodies with three main parts and six walking legs.

Both insects and arachnids have exoskeletons. The outer covering of their bodies and legs is hard. It protects the soft, inner parts of their bodies.

a ladybird

delicate wing

hard wing case

This spider's body is protected by its exoskeleton.

a spider

Some arachnids' **exoskeletons** are fierce weapon systems. For example, a scorpion's tail has sections that act like **joints**. While the scorpion holds its prey with its pincers, its tail curls up and delivers a deadly sting.

Another type of arachnid, called a tarantula, might look soft and furry, but it still has an exoskeleton. The hard covering over each leg is divided into seven segments, or parts. This makes the tarantula flexible.

As a tarantula grows, it moults, or sheds, its exoskeleton from time to time.

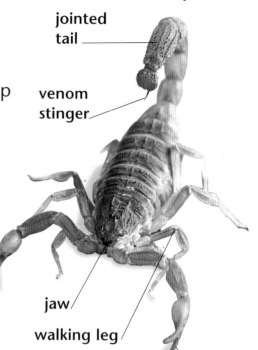

desert scorpion

jointed tail

venom stinger

jaw

walking leg

pincer

tarantula's old exoskeleton

tarantula

Insects such as beetles are protected by a tough, waterproof exoskeleton. Adult beetles have more of this armour than any other kind of insect. Some even have pointed spikes and horns. All beetles also have hard wing cases that cover their wings. They open these wing cases to fly.

A Beetle Takes Flight

1 This beetle is about to fly into the air.

2 It grips the plant while the hard wing cases begin to open.

3 Its hard wing cases spread out and the thin, delicate wings open and begin to move.

4 The beetle glides through the air.

The Growth of a Damselfly

Young insects change in size and shape as they grow up. Some kinds of young insects, such as young damselflies, dragonflies and grasshoppers, change shape gradually each time they moult, or shed their **exoskeleton**. Young insects like these are known as nymphs. This change in shape is called **metamorphosis**.

1 The nymph rests on a stem.

2 The nymph grows, and the skin splits.

3 The nymph is now an adult. It breaks free of the exoskeleton.

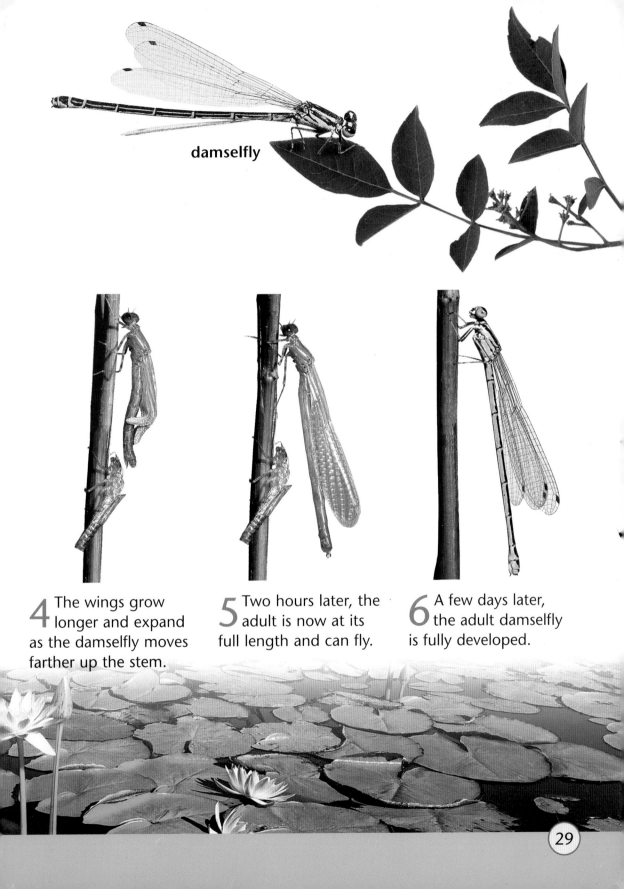

damselfly

4 The wings grow longer and expand as the damselfly moves farther up the stem.

5 Two hours later, the adult is now at its full length and can fly.

6 A few days later, the adult damselfly is fully developed.

Skeletons All Over

Skeletons are very important as they support the body's weight and protect the organs of the body, such as the brain.

Skeletons give animals the power to walk, climb, swim or jump. A fish's skeleton, for example, gives it the power to swim through water. Without our skeletons, we would not be able to pick up a pen, jump or dance to music. What would you do without your skeleton?

Glossary

amphibians	cold-blooded animals that have a spine and that live on land and in water
cartilage	a strong, flexible tissue that forms a skeleton or connects parts of the skeleton
crustacean	an animal that has a hard outer shell and that usually lives in water
endoskeleton	the firm, supportive and protective structure found inside the body of some animals
exoskeleton	a hard, outer covering on some animals that provides support and protection
extinct	no longer in existence; species of animal or plant that has died out
fossils	bones, teeth and other remains of animals or plants that lived long ago
joints	any of the places where two bones come together
mammals	warm-blooded animals that have a spine and fur or hair; mothers produce milk for their young
metamorphosis	the process through which some animals change in size and shape from birth to adulthood
skull	the bony framework of the head that protects the brain
spine	backbone; also a thin, sharp-pointed part that sticks out from some animals or plants
sternum	a long bone in the chest that connects to the ribs and bones in the shoulders; also called a *breastbone*
vertebrae	(singular, **vertebra**) the small bones that make up the spine

Index